AMERICAN GIRL

New Issues Poetry & Prose

Editor	Herbert Scott
Copy Editors	Eric Hansen, Jonathan Pugh
Readers	Kirsten Hemmy, Adela Najarro, Margaret von Steinen, Cody Todd
Assistants to the Editor	Rebecca Beech, Lynnea Page, Marianne E. Swierenga
Business Manager	Michele McLaughlin
Fiscal Officer	Marilyn Rowe

New Issues Poetry & Prose
The College of Arts and Sciences
Western Michigan University
Kalamazoo, MI 49008

An Inland Seas Poetry Book

 Inland Seas poetry books are supported by a grant from
The Michigan Council for Arts and Cultural Affairs.

First Edition, 2004.

ISBN   1-930974-30-2 (paperbound)

Library of Congress Cataloging-in-Publication Data:
Cory, Cynie
American Girl/Cynie Cory
Library of Congress Control Number: 2003104649

Art Director	Tricia Hennessy
Designer	Dana Killinger
Production Manager	Paul Sizer
	The Design Center, Department of Art
	College of Fine Arts
	Western Michigan University

AMERICAN GIRL

CYNIE CORY

New Issues

WESTERN MICHIGAN UNIVERSITY

Cynie Cory's best poems inventively recast ideas of gender and American experience. Many are notable for their mosaic-like phrases, and for their unexpected remarks on the making of self-as-other. It's exciting that we may not know whether the lines are meant to be intimate or public—the whisper meets the shout. Whatever it means to be an American Girl is beautifully reordered here.

—Brenda Hillman

for my mother, to the memory of my mother

Contents

III. American Girl

Acknowledgments

I gratefully acknowledge the editors of the following publications, in which many of these poems, occasionally in different form, first appeared:

The American Poetry Review: "American Sky," "Everything About Winter," "The Importance of Angels," "Moon/Mirror," "The Plum Tree: Self-Portrait," "Sequel," "The Terminology of Winter (How the Past Exists)," "What Is America?"

Apalachee Quarterly: "To Tell a Story (Cleaning Fish)"

The Bitter Oleander: "The Smell of Snow"

The Café Review: "The Intruder"

The Indiana Review: "Fishing"

Literal Latté: "Dominion"

The North American Review: "Self-Portrait as Janis Joplin"

Pequod: "from *The Paradise Diary*"

The Pittsburgh Quarterly: "The Fiction"

The Quarterly: "Clink into the Arms of America," "The Theory of Everything"

Shenandoah: "On Pierre Cecile Puvis De Chavannes (1824-1898) Untitled (Twilight)"

Willow Springs: "There is a Thing Called"

I would like to thank Barbara Hamby for her generous care in the shaping of this manuscript, for her encouragement from the early stages of this project, and for her vision, all of which have been necessary for its completion. I would also like to thank Brenda Hillman for giving the manuscript its final touches, and for selecting it. Thanks to Brigitte Byrd for her intelligent suggestions, especially during the final revisions of the poems. My deepest gratitude to Herb Scott for believing in this manuscript from the start. And especially to my mother, who always knew.

She sounded amusing—a typical, high-spirited American girl.

—Paul Bowles,
The Sheltering Sky

I.

Everything About Winter

Iceberg

I can't swallow the distance
it has traveled without a jar. Nervous and glass-like,
it clinks without sophistication,
pulses to the slow tempo of night
like an afterthought grown cold, lingering,
half-surfaced, a swollen witness.

I cannot budge the iceberg. It is locked inside my skull
like a form of etiquette.

The Smell of Snow

The eyelash moon returns to the black above this city where I don't recognize the sound of my favorite song.   In a desert you carry me across broken waves.   I am dying, loving you like this.   My heart is a cave burdened by distance.   But in this movie we tear each other open, we devour flesh as though we are harnessed by nothing.   I own the impossibility of you.   I own the shape of your shoulders, the pulse of your neck.   I lose my breath under stars I have tried to rearrange.

We are on this journey fueled by night.   Because I have given myself to work I lose sight of you.   I call for you repeatedly.   I wait among the turnstiles in the subterranean dark.   You appear with a memory coded by afterthoughts.   I try to crack it, to penetrate your deliverance.   There is so much at stake, we have lost the will to speak.   —   You are so far from here, walking in tall grass, rhyming your verbs.   I drift north.

The Intruder

1

Like the saints before her, my sister did not speak.
He used a six-inch buck knife.
I could not see her face. I wanted to.
I'd cut off my right arm but I can't.

2

When we escaped we escaped as girls.
I ran, my nightgown hit my calves like a horse's tail.
We could not see what was before us.

3

Something about my mother. When I see her
the pain strangles me. I watch.

I pretend I cannot hear.

4

Someone inspects my period as though I've committed a crime.
I bury myself in beach sand until I am no longer ready.
It is debatable whether I am American.
I decide to flee to Paris for no artistic reason.

5

I fired my father's .410 shotgun when I was ten.
It ripped apart my intelligence.

I began believing in ammunition, in passion, in the right to
                                        take possession.

6

From my father, I learned to dream,
and from his dreams, collapsed
and disfigured, I pressed time
into a lyric, prescribed to me by no one.

The Fiction

This is the context for that which it is.
You are—say you are the river I am walking along,
these pine trees' pine cones
staring me in the arteries like antlers I have seen
roadside in the dark in the dark the deer fear these white eyes
oh—it is slowing, double-time, this dysfunctional scene—

twisting in the dam of branches are the road maps drifting—having
drifted, once a rough draft of ship made of the most articulate vision.

I am walking beside you, river, that only I see as I walk
beside you in the crescent of my eye a future still responding
to multiple seizures, this current is survival, I am pulling
toward you toward each bend I might respect, I can see

onward, this same unified plight: say you never
would be a river, never was or even let me manipulate you into being
one of those continuous seizures—okay, I am not a permanent
fixture at your side of bone meal, I never planted these trees

nor did you resist me when I moved in closer to your drivel . . .
I am drifting beside, you who are not you nor the river I expect
                                              you to believe in.
I am this context we can believe in for awhile, or forever or for
                                              ever how long
you think fiction will last.

Gun

Inside the camera's eye I grew to love
exquisite detail, glorious and horrifying.
I examined the angel stalking the hunter.
I believed Jesus was a madman desiring luck.
I watched my father's hands rip the duck's feather from its back.
Of America, I knew about winter.
How everything around me disappeared
at the mouth of the river behind my father's house.
I sank to the iced-over lake

and sang my song to the disappearing angel o.

The Terminology of Winter (How The Past Exists)

The river behind my father's only house opens its mouth like moaning
into the lake. Every winter it freezes there like that, open.
Underneath, what flows never rests, tormented, the terror of everything
        past and present—
How many bodies are trapped? Winter never really finishes itself. When
        the surface cracks.

When the ice breaks free. It is still winter.

       *   *   *   *

Icebergs from an aerial view got no soul, no flower—it's the
                                       underneath that counts.
You should see it—all that space
between the jello-hardness and the inseparable sky—

Blue is the in-between that jets forgiveness
for the whatever it is we can't put our hard hats to—you know the odor,
it's a veritable eggshell. It's a

not-breathing in the air rush—the pressure
of the in-between, the worry, the itchy mess

(those lovely icebergs)—the arrangement of angles perishing
into a fit of foam, of blue into purity—a clearlessness into
some kind of clear—a dumpster overflowing

a sudden turn around the corner of a humid darkness—
                                   (after twilight)
after sun blimps its way into a burial ground for lifetimes—
                                  how planets run
their gamut and back off into the far reaches—like they don't exist.

And we're not stupid. We don't like to be fuel
for some kind of humor.

*　　　　*　　　　*　　　　*

(So it was, in my mind . . . an afterthought.) I was born

under a foreign blanket of hieroglyphics, etched inside a swarming

aurora borealis. I saw it once. Each time a newness occurred.
A gathering of infant stones—pebbles on the beach under a
flabby moon.

Those waves out there were bodies melting. Into each other.
Darknesses

folding. I never underestimated

the terrific wind pulling in the dark caps, driftwood

at my feet, appeared. (Canada.) This is what I heard:

a landscape like this could not love me. Out there in the night vision

I saw my soul take a wide shadow over the pockets of darkness,
at my feet

drifted the bodies mangled—I saw

other worlds. Other light, not the light from the separating moon, no

light from the shackled stars, footprints in a white white snow

where my body must have been. Had I walked

in the direction of the North Star—where it beckoned

on the edge of the peninsula, North? It was my downfall, my

imagination zinging into colder claims for reasons

—North is a box full of lost mothers, never fathers, only the same face,

the same insincere calculation—fingers penetrating the surface

of an iced-over lake.   On my back I listened

to the black sky stiffen. *Waiting.* I released what I knew of the
                                        constellations:

Venus there somewhere between where the horizon
                    once was, where the horizon

must be an arc of snowfall . . . my eyes cold, as if the glistening
                                        of white gold

were everything I attempted to become. (How did I get here?)
                                        Locked
        in the black-

ness—packed into ice and snow, my breath, I could see it, form
                                                into a
        disappearing . . .

I wanted everything back. The stars. The clouds. The bodies
                                        stuck
        beneath the frozen lake.

The water from my eyes slowed like blood and, eventually, dried—
                                        my lashes,

the pulse of my temples, like dying, clicked into ice.

There is a Thing Called

There is a thing in madness
which is rivers. Rivers
and rows of live oaks, dangling
Spanish moss reflecting the tide.

There is a dock and there is a father at the end of the dock.
In the river are trees. Lifetimes of trees.
There is a smell of fire in the trees.

There is a thing called by a name which eludes the speaker;
The speaker is somewhere in the river.
Imagine the speaker as the river which is on fire with the
                                    trees of madness.

The dock is a broken branch
in the eye of the river
which is the eye of God
which is the other thing the speaker can't remember.

Fishing

My father and I, in an aluminum rowboat, with Hershey bars and
    sandwiches stuffed in our pockets,
would sit breathing icy air into our waking lungs, the sun not yet
    breaking the horizon, the time
when quiet is the lapping, soft against the boat, the oars dipping
    the sound of forgiveness.
My father, stern and lean, beautiful in the eyes of women, untouchable
    in my own, held onto the oars
with his long ready hands, a pipe in his mouth, moustache forming
    ice, eyebrows furrowed like mine.
Everything was serious, a philosophy, a destiny, a pulsing quiet with
    my wool hat pulled to my ears,
the schnapps in a flask, hugging my father's breast, waiting for the
    celebration of the first fish,
the first real fish I ever caught, not the little Bluegills or Sunfish with
    my sister, the ones
we always threw back because of their size, because I didn't want to
    kill them anyway, the summer
I first remember hating my father for humiliating my mother, the
    summer he chased her with a snake
out of the cottage, while she cried hysterically, he laughed hysterically,
    my mother loving him
until he made her crack, like how he made me crack, how I thought
    the pole was going to crack, snap
in half while my father watched me struggling to keep the line from
    giving, yelling *Dad, help!*
almost crying, begging, panicking, and he wouldn't help, he said *Do
    it yourself,* and I hated him,
afraid I would fail because he wanted me to win, and that fish made
    me hate him, that goddamn fish, 21 inches
long and beautiful, flopping in the net, slick colors glistening in the
    cold sun, and he made me take it
off the hook, rip its gills, drag the silver metal through its beautiful
    mouth, tearing its flesh,

and he made me stick a knife in its silver belly, plump with
    spawn, and he was so pleased we had bait
for more killing, and I felt the cold blood flushing into my
    hands, organs slipping through my fingers,
the steam of my breath in the air, and the sweet, putrid smell
    of escaping life flaring my nose
like that, like a hungry dog, and he poured the schnapps, no,
    he gave me a swig because I was
such a sport and he was so proud. I was beaming, despite my
    hate, despite my fear, and the schnapps
was my friend, so I asked for more, *just one more,* I would say,
    and we drank while his stern hazel eyes
watched the movement of my throat with the liquor going down,
    and I asked for another, like my mother,
until he refused, and his eyes, I remember the white, made me
    feel his disgust, made me hate his fear,
and I didn't understand my desire, I only knew I needed to wash
    away the blood drying tight on my hands,
and to sleep without nightmares, and to try to understand, or
    forget, or not really believe, why I
have to perform, catching fish.

To Tell a Story (Cleaning Fish)

I misunderstood everything. I was perpendicular to it.
My dad was a boy he was like he was
naked in his clothes in white dry waves the floor was
spread out, wet then, after the silver messages rang from the gills.
My mother was with him maybe maybe she was somewhere else like
                                                                    it was
daylight or something there was no definite edge like the fresh cut
herbs beside the knife in a glass of water absorbed this strange light
as if it were everything flushed out undressed as if it were meant to
hold everything as if it were the first time this light ever fell this way
to earth in a single predicament articulate stretching itself repeating
                                                            itself it kept
repeating itself like that until you could smell everything in the
                                                            newspapers
the blood the rage the absolute purity of knowing it happened like *that.*

Ice Age: History

Within the holocaust of shame I grew
to hate my body, its ransomed poise false
in his hands: a bird stunned before it falls
from the limb of a tree; my heart moved
beyond the amputated moon, seduced
by authority's self-logic, a waltz
where time undresses her, presses—a pulse
that repulses, the body refuses
itself. Long-distance, road-weary, travels
through valleys that are nothing but glaciers.
O! To smash them with a thousand gavels,
obliterate flesh! Will this erase her?
Save her from what history now unravels?
She cannot escape what shapes her anger.

Clink into the Arms of America

Measure emptiness by the plate glass smashed
she said to herself, forget the coffee
out loud. Fucking mother, what am I, gashed
across America, can't you see? Sloppy
is my trail, naked and run-down. Hoping
for those dark eyes, I search minefields blank, wrong.
There's a cactus in my heart exploding
with the storm clouds. I simply have no song,
Lord! I destroy the tune for any house.
Jam-packed w/ nicotine fingers, I fight
the jagged edges. I strip the fat grouse
wingless, I rip them, guiltless, from their flight.

I'm a target for the interruption.
I'm a shotgun silencing discussion.

Sequel

Pardon my lips she said without rami-
fications this begins the fictions of
self as one lone cell selectively lost
in cheap molecular memory, his-
tory competitive as the diffi-
cult desire to terminate what's caught
between her legs with force this holocaust
denial, dream. Here is the mortar lis-
ten can you breathe, dear? O mother, cover
me in kisses, put me in the ground, seize
no other moment. The blizzard's over.
I don't remember the dishrags, but please,
the body doesn't lie. How you smother
me in distance. I camouflage this freeze.

Everything About Winter

I love the thorny rose with the sun through its skin
The red skin
The water below

This woman whom I idolized and dreamed about for years
Put my head in her lap where I could smell her

I let her take me.
I wanted her to confuse me—

I said "We'll always have Paris" before the termination of
                                        our preconsummation

She felt the calluses on my palms rough her arms gently

There were no camels under the light of forgetting

It was smooth silent unrushed.

        In the sense that there was no deliverance

I felt glory and hope but I despised the furniture.

She was lonely but I knew she had everything

        inside her, I never got there

There was deceit

        which I meant to her, with my American hands

sowing the grains of rye into a dry flat land before us.

She remembered everything about winter
        how I was winter
In a white T-shirt tanned and beautiful she said

There was a wooden lake between us and we never arrived.

For centuries we wish to walk across.

II.

Under a Theatre of Stars

The Plum Tree: Self-Portrait

Last night among the smell of mothballs I vanished into the dark
$\qquad\qquad\qquad\qquad\qquad\qquad\qquad\qquad$purple
$\qquad\qquad$blackness of plums, the plums of my youth, the plums my
$\qquad\qquad\qquad\qquad\qquad\qquad\qquad\qquad$father let drop
$\qquad\qquad$from the drooping limbs into the handfuls of overgrown grass.

It was dark. (Of the thickness of the drooping limbs.)
There was nothing but the sound of the falling fruit.
The lake pulled the cold hard granules of sand over colder
$\qquad\qquad\qquad\qquad\qquad\qquad\qquad\qquad$rounder pebbles—

How could I wander through the bruised night? The stars were
$\qquad\qquad\qquad\qquad\qquad\qquad\qquad\qquad$islands of light
$\qquad\qquad\qquad$telling me about the smallness of me,
$\qquad\qquad\qquad\qquad\qquad\qquad\qquad$the *smallness*

$\qquad\qquad\qquad\qquad$—a fracture of light, a failure
$\qquad\qquad\qquad\qquad\qquad\qquad\qquad\qquad$of science

I wanted to—*I wished to*—to $\qquad\qquad\qquad$create a darkness *around*
$\qquad\qquad\qquad\qquad\qquad\qquad\qquad\qquad$the light,
$\qquad\qquad\qquad\qquad\qquad$to squeeze

$\qquad$the wordless images from the night.

My lips sang words no one heard. These words drifted shapeless $\qquad$31
$\qquad$from the swollen mouth

then a *roundness* forming no sound . . .

$\qquad\qquad\qquad\qquad$The moon was indifferent.
$\qquad\qquad\qquad\qquad$The moon swallowed itself.

$\qquad$The whole sky shattered into a black field.

The stars wept, disappeared

like this song I am lifting from my wooden lungs:

The Importance of Angels

There was a spotlight that suffocated us.
I couldn't decide whether it deceived us.
It was the eternal blizzard, non-accepting of Jesus.
Like I was raised in this hermetic ritual of murders.
Like a horrific nightmare of seizure, the indifference was solitude.
A form of wishing I've never been.
Was there a murder? Were we self-sacrificed?
Is the idea to pretend we are born to deceive?

I decided I was not to discuss this.
I would see stars in the center of the black room.
It was not to be reckoned with.

*

I used to believe I was a fragment, a visitor, a lucky idiot.

On Pierre Cecile Puvis de Chavannes (1824-1898)
Untitled (Twilight)

Oh, God, the man is weeping, having just read
half the bible left open like the forced petals
of a rose beside a rock, he slumps in his own
debris. He has trembled far, lost his wife, children,
to the stiff black muscle of winter. Purple and brown
mix to blood sledged across his whole purpose. Even the cold moon
digs its round edges into the weird blue sky.
Beyond the surface tension lies a dream inside a dream,
a distinct mountain reminds the figure of his losses.
The sea at his feet becomes enormous, hardening white
at its edges like an icy moustache, icy eyes, icy breath
round the mouth. There is no reason to go or stay. The darkness
is a false shelter around his shoulders like emerging wings
cracking where the light splits. The shadow on the foreground
is Jesus dying and not rising.

from *The Paradise Diary*

I am talking about the 20th century,
I am talking about myself.
It is 1:10 pm, I have lost my lover,
Delta plane crash in Texas, the news displays the rummage, mangled
Bodies charred, helicopters swarming in on an hallucination.

It is trouble in Paradise.
I go into one bathroom, the next.
I move to a cactus where ants play gin rummy.
Poison is air.
Last night it rained the worst since Hurricane Klaus.
My lover, I held her like a crocodile in my arms, dreaming
Kingdoms, kidneys, the cancer probe into the left ventricle bone
                                                    scraped
Stripped clean forming sweet sloppy marrow, she came
In my mouth.

———————

I cannot hold onto this sadness any longer.
I have been staring impatiently at the hibiscus,
the faded orange bothers my eyesight.
It seems I have been unable to see the pattern,
white caps coming into harbor, out there, my view.

The wind chimes forgive, forgive.
A distant car muffles ocean or birds or rain.

A lizard scampers, hesitates.
It is young. A fly escapes.

———————

Today I swam inside a fish.
Actually, the fish carried me—
it swam, I floated
like a lobster without a guard-rail.
There were swarms of jellyfish,
they turned their transparent,
purpley bodies over, over, folding
within the dreamy waves, they were flowers.
We went far, almost flying,
saw a stingray—so huge
& flat—a tail longer
than a giraffe neck.

———————

I can't write about my home town.

I've discovered memories in Caribbean mosquitoes.

I scrape a machete against a leathery eggshell.

An iguana is busy being born.

I want to die on a country road, listening to thunder.

Where there are rows of birch trees and acres of sundown.

I will sleep past the last road-sign pointing northward.

I grew up in a graveyard listening to nothing.

I was so afraid of dying I began again.

The Country I Cannot Enter

If I live to touch her, I will cure the cold.
It's common, how you maximize forgiveness
like a shortcut to the store.

Just south of Georgia's border I lick the milkshake from my lip,
watch the waitress check her slip.

It's up to me. She's forgotten
how glorious is the road,
how I improve it, smash the dashboard like a sun.

Tell her how far I've come to where I was not before.
How far it takes to become lost, nothing
like a Chinese theatre, glamorous and masked.

I see with eyes like a gun, unreasonable,
gray ice, the price of betrayal.
If you go away I will find you

by the shell of a familiar moon,
inside the tenor of an obscured promise.

Locating the Unified Field

1. Through mine fields I step, lay down my arsenal.

2. No theory can explain good intentions.

3. The criminal moon exhausts itself.

4. I memorize the silence of my barricade.

5. I don't mind being lost among the rubble.

6. I will remember you under a theatre of stars.

7. Your eyes were my philosophy.

8. I have recovered the will to let you go.

*

The snow falls like science.

      (Elegant as a proof.)

I dream I hold the equation that will save us.

      [I arrange my apology around me and laugh.]

In America I won't look back.

Wildflowers

O listen! The wind reaches for us
as though we are lost

      *

How could you know what words to say
you don't even know what moves me

      *

There are answers in the wind
I have listened and I have heard

      *

I walk across this distance, America

      *

I was born under the warring courage of hieroglyphics
I trust the sound of your voice

      *

There were visitors I could not see
Metal was the color of the crippled light

      *

Rock-a-bye baby, don't say a word
I swallow a mockingbird

      *

Frame me, mirror. Night is war.
I am cradled by cracks in the floor.

*

Summer fails like a ruptured moon
Under a broken fan I begin again

*

O beautiful, O graceful girl
I don't know what to do

Fall on Me

There are no plum trees reaching for us tonight.

No moon caught in the fence.

Your lips are swollen like dark rose petals pulsing outward,

flames giving light to the shadows of plums.

How gracefully we step over them; it is our art.

Girl, I beg you to leave your country.

The moon here is practical, innocuous. I have seen it

slice open the throat of a grieving woman while she wept in the street.

*

I dream of you repeatedly. I am a field and you are (in me)

               looking for home.

But you don't see, your eyes flutter like two moths against the light.

Lie down in these pastures, I can afford to wear your bones.   **41**

*

I push into you without theory, without speaking.

I kiss the entire mouth of you like a moon I swallow in the hurry.

Your wrist slips over my eye where I see beyond the flesh of you:

the lonely childhood, the poems half-written.

*

I am with you like a blistered angel caught in the light.

(It was a Cuban moon, it was smoke that came my way.)

How could you take cover? Turn from the orchards that have bathed
you for centuries

in rubble. I uncover a wooden nail, clench it in my fist while I travel

under a moon that swears it will.

Dominion

Under the skull of a fallen star, shall I ever shatter
the distance between us, the orchard of plum trees, rows
ripened and purple, bending branches

in the naked moon of a mind

touching you every way, the way

grass beneath us cools

what is changed, what is really not changed?

The plum of your lips.

The plum of your throat.

The plum of your wrist.

The plum of your kiss.

III.

American Girl

Moon/Mirror

Tonight you will be egotistical.
You will rip apart an orange into the sects of the moon's forms
Torn there, shattered framed by the instant magnet of hardness
It's equivalent to a formula—a formulation for destruction
An elliptical theory in a fit of an angelic disorder in disputable
                                              earth tones
Each starry night without blundering, completely voluptuous like
                      science like hurling words not theory
Inside this mirror-insight, this near-ice like God resisting temptation
                      facing a hard-shaved river
Is anyone out there listening? I've rubbed these same two stars
                      together now for centuries shuddering
Into the ordinary slivered sky a private sigh unravels:
What do you want to know? A lilting negative honoring?

Self-Portrait as Janis Joplin

I make a decision to drive it in
like the blues, throaty and lusty, to soothe
the current range of exposure. Listen,
there's no resistance, no error to prove
I am a steeple without dominion.
The distance destroys me like a sleeve blurred
long after hours. Beyond opinion
I cope with desire like grief worded
inexactly. I want oblivion
like a girl wants a Barbie doll. I face
the stage and enter the insistence, young
and full of grace. I arrive to escape

like the heart of a chord strung out, in flames.
For the life of me, I don't know your names.

Back Home in America

There is nothing about America

Mexican, African, come up to me

like a slashed wrist, asking me

what's wrong under a sky set to bomb

caskets jamming streets and interstate

a hit parade in the temple of my pulse

dog breath, axle grease, I find a cash machine

There's a God in all of us

like a target, like an abstract song

I'm going to marry a plumber, an organ grinder

I'm going to sing along

American Girl

1

My eyes rivet to the rearview mirror, her dress is in a hurry.
On my knees I hammer her excuses like I am her
American hypocrisy.
It's futile.   She's a disaster.   An equation I revert to
in a moment of history.   Her sleeves slip.
I claim her throat.   Like an architect she
unveils me.   I can't pretend.
I know the score.
We've grown to be each other's whore.

2

I have risen under an amputated moon.
I have walked across a moment that will not break.
Under a latex sky I hold a grain of wisdom, a separate vision
like a lucky star that falls from position.

O take my famous hips and empty me with precision.

Map & Legend, Circa 1998 (American)

The wind unattended, I drink full-throated

here in the warm South, sick for home, that North star

serious, murmuring *cross rivers and flat lands.*

How is it my shadow is not enough? I cannot leave her,

silence like metal on my tongue. Chaos is my heart.

I am smothered by constellations. I travel North.

Where else does one start? At the end of the day.

What is America?

She lay on me, my head on her—I had fallen far from the great
north woods to her

Southern cross. Could I point it out to you? She wore a fuse
around her neck &

I fantasized she was some beautiful boy in the Army Reserve.
Then she took my head

I found—my tongue like a soft wet blade parting her.

This wealth around me. Jolting me into another oblivion.

Under the crisp white sheets I turned, ribbing away from
her toward

Where another voice wanted me. Moon, O! Moon I scream at
voluminous memories

In my sleep a thousand sleepers walk.

*

Take my hand. O beautiful one. Hug me tight to the stars,

Heart of many grains.

American Rhetoric

In a landscape like this, we deserve sleep.

Roughly estimated, I can't contact Venus without a discourse.

Go. Drive this hearse past the last satellite.

It's futile. The fist on the dash.

The ice that won't freeze us.

The ghost of X lights a match.

Nobody hits the ground.

(I can't say this.)

Nobody sounds distressed.

In an elevator, I'm going down.

You play the piano wearing gloves.

Look at me, you say, *we are invisible.*

Shelve the cans of tuna, stack the bottled water.

In earnest, the theatre is all we have.

Glorious as a rainbow.

Figurative as lust.

The Smell of Gasoline

Amputate the moon like a theory that strings us together.
Time insists we murder fear like a country, fill our days with
                                        bones, hash, amphetamines.

Your eyes smash molecules, rivet me into strange religions.
(A tide on fire, a blanket of oyster shells.)

(A moon throws itself into the formica.)
(I hold a coma in my hands.)

(Behind you is a mirror that won't reflect us.)
(Behind you is a field I can't caress.)

Is the soul a liar? Have you tasted fear like a gun?
(I wear words on my sleeve like a conversation I cannot hum.)

Tell me there is a God for all of us.
In my fiction you are balanced on a string.

We cross the unified field as though it is a river in America.

American Sky

How can I turn back toward the pearl moon
punctured into the pale dusk winter blue?
How can I turn back?
How can I turn back?
Moon, statue of promise, flesh-moon immune

to my loneliness: follow me—will you?
Round moon caught between these limbs' blackening hue.
How can I turn back?
How can I turn back?
Almost perfect, like the thumb's print pressed huge.

Might I be your lover if I refuse
this world of distance, clip its edges through?
How can I turn back?
How can I turn back?
Can you comfort me, oh ice-silent moon?

All this darkness falling around us will soon
cover me completely and we will move—
(How can I turn back?)
(How can I turn back?)
further in distance. For in distance you

carry that body: universe, and loom
from that black pocket. *Nothing* is your view.
How can I turn back?
How can I turn back?
I shall memorize, in this light's form, *you*.

95 South, Georgia

Shoved past the moon driving deeper south
Night gnawed on us, my nerves shredded
like I was listening to speed guitars and screaming heads
I no longer was resilient
My bones ached, the stars became brittle
Don't worry about the universe, said a voice,
This is all you have.

I made the decision to leave America, the music no longer
my culture—the violence betrayed me—
Deep in my heart I knew I was an expatriate
Who telephoned me? Who had the vision?
I would like to have leapt for all to see
to no longer be invisible, to be a swift-moving target

For the theatre to collect its tickets under me
For Time to click from one moment to the next
without taking everything back.

The Theory of Everything

I.

There is a God.

He wants a flower the size of Philadelphia
        to open in the moonlight
even when the moonlight
        is dirty.

The universe is something I can believe in.
It can't be defined by roundness

it folds into darknesses dragging currents
that breathe   it goes back into

its self.

All the mothers and fathers of the night sitting bedside
outside windows, behind scratchy jukeboxes,

liquor oozes down multiple throats

soars over the back steps of wooden apart-
ments, —— staring strangely at the moon.

—the moon listens and breathes

        into houses—

            taking responsibility

for the sad kisses, the broken windows.

II.

Charlie, jazz is everything

I ever wanted:

> An everything; it includes
>
> a never-leaving, it holds
>
> the notes
>
> even in silence.

III.

The overlapping hands of the ten dimensions is impossible
                                         to comprehend.

I can't even envision:

> the light from each broken star that hides

the mother the father

the indiscriminate lovers ——

> A straight line they can walk across

A second line perpendicular

The place jazz passes

where light does not exist.

How fire parts air and slips

into the past,   How fire exists

in the leaving—

A porch door swinging

An empty house   where everything is a dark bird singing—

The father the mother come together to *stay* they say:

We want to leave the door open he was playing *so* pretty.

photo by Barbara Hamby

Cynie Cory grew up in Marquette, Michigan. She is a graduate of the Iowa Writers' Workshop and Florida State University, where she earned a Ph.D. Her poetry has appeared in *The American Poetry Review*, *Another Chicago Magazine*, *Black Warrior Review*, *Crazyhorse*, *New American Writing*, *Shade*, *Verse* and *Western Humanities Review*. She currently teaches writing and literature at FSU in Tallahassee, Florida.

New Issues Poetry & Prose

Editor, Herbert Scott

Sarah Mangold, *Household Mechanics*
Gail Martin, *The Hourglass Heart*
David Marlatt, *A Hog Slaughtering Woman*
Gretchen Mattox, *Goodnight Architecture*
Paula McLain, *Less of Her*
Sarah Messer, *Bandit Letters*
Malena Mörling, *Ocean Avenue*
Julie Moulds, *The Woman with a Cubed Head*
Gerald Murnane, *The Plains* (fiction)
Marsha de la O, *Black Hope*
C. Mikal Oness, *Water Becomes Bone*
Elizabeth Powell, *The Republic of Self*
Margaret Rabb, *Granite Dives*
Rebecca Reynolds, *Daughter of the Hangnail; The Bovine Two-Step*
Martha Rhodes, *Perfect Disappearance*
Beth Roberts, *Brief Moral History in Blue*
John Rybicki, *Traveling at High Speeds* (enlarged second edition)
Mary Ann Samyn, *Inside the Yellow Dress*
Ever Saskya, *The Porch is a Journey Different From the House*
Mark Scott, *Tactile Values*
Martha Serpas, *Côte Blanche*
Diane Seuss-Brakeman, *It Blows You Hollow*
Elaine Sexton, *Sleuth*
Marc Sheehan, *Greatest Hits*
Sarah Jane Smith, *No Thanks—and Other Stories* (fiction)
Phillip Sterling, *Mutual Shores*
Angela Sorby, *Distance Learning*
Russell Thorburn, *Approximate Desire*
Rodney Torreson, *A Breathable Light*
Robert VanderMolen, *Breath*
Martin Walls, *Small Human Detail in Care of National Trust*
Patricia Jabbeh Wesley, *Before the Palm Could Bloom: Poems of Africa*